FAITH OF THE FOREIGN SOLDIER

THIERRY BOYA
AND ELISE DISMER

ENTEGRITY
CHOICE PUBLISHING

Entegrity Choice Publishing
PO Box 453 Powder Springs, GA 30127
info@entegritypublishing.com
www.entegritypublishing.com
404.472.9190

Printed in the United States of America

ISBN: 979-8-9850792-7-2

Library of Congress Control Number: 2024906732

Foreword

Thierry Boya, originally from Ivory Coast, is a member of World Harvest Church. He has a passion for God, and the Holy Spirit has used him to give insight to himself and others. He truly is a man of the Spirit. I have known him to receive words from the Lord in visions and dreams on a repeated basis.

His life is a testimony of a walk of faith. When people would speak negatively about his life and future, he would rise up and believe the Word that God had spoken to him for promotion and success. No one thought he could ever get out of his role working at Fresh Market and become a soldier in the U.S. Army. However, through his dreams and the leading of the Spirit, he is now a U.S. Army soldier.

His story is a strong encouragement for all those who are seeking to follow God's plan for their life. If you will read his testimony, you will be encouraged and receive faith to lean into the voice of God and His leading into the supernatural and watch God take you to new places you thought were impossible. Truly his testimony is about what Jesus said, "With man this is impossible, but with God all things are possible." Matthew 19:25 (NIV)

Pastor Mirek Hufton

Acknowledgments

A s I turn the pages of this journey that culminated in the creation of this book, I am filled with profound gratitude to the Lord Jesus and a deep sense of appreciation for what have been the pillars of support, guidance, and inspiration in my life.

To my family, who have been my unwavering foundation—your love, belief, and sacrifices have shaped the person I am today. Your encouragement has been the wind beneath my wings, propelling me forward, even in the face of adversity.

To my friends, who have been a source of endless joy, laughter, and comfort—your companionship on this journey has been invaluable. In moments of doubt, your faith in me has been a guiding light, illuminating my path.

To my mentors, my spiritual father Pastor Djonfene Jean Jacques, Pastor Mirek and colleagues, and Prophet David Aimee Jeremy, whose wisdom and insights have profoundly influenced my growth and learning—your guidance has been instrumental in honing my skills and shaping my thoughts. I am deeply thankful for your vital contributions to my professional and personal development.

To my writer, Elise Dismer, who heard my stories in French and wove them together in English—the Lord will use your gift with words mightily.

To those who have touched my life in various capacities, leaving indelible marks on my journey—your impact may have been brief, but its significance is deeply etched into my heart.

This book is not only a reflection of my efforts but also a tapestry woven with the threads of all your contributions, support, and faith. It stands as a testament to the incredible power of community, love, and shared dreams. From the bottom of my heart, thank you for being a part of my story.

Contents

Introduction

As a young boy growing up in Ivory Coast in West Africa, I never would have dreamed of the life I live now. I never would have imagined the good plans God had for me: of living in America, happily married, speaking a whole new language, and walking with purpose as a father and as a member of the U.S. Army. In this book, I share the story of how God accomplished these plans, how He made His presence known to me, and how remarkably He fulfilled His promises in my life.

Faith of the Foreign Soldier is a book that will truly encourage you. It is written so that you would desire a deeper relationship with Jesus Christ and expand what you think is possible in your life and relationship with God. This book is filled with examples of how the impossibilities of man become possible with God. The same Holy Spirit who has moved the mountains in my life can move the mountains in your life.

I share stories from my life in this book that demonstrate how faithful God has been to me . . . miracle after miracle. I hope your desire to deepen your relationship with Him abounds within you. I know how wonderfully my life has changed as a result of following Jesus, and I desire that same joy for you. May the Lord encourage you deeply as you read the rest of this book!

CHAPTER 1
A Curious Storm

knew I needed to go to church. I had never been before, but a Christian man who kept knocking on my door had told me about Jesus and about Heaven and Hell. The fear of going to Hell had started to grip me.

Still, I wanted my chance to party one last time before starting that new, "moral" life the next day. After all, it was Saturday night, and I was seventeen, a young man ready to hit the streets of Danané, Ivory Coast, with my cousin. We had our night all planned out.

Yet as we started to walk to the clubs, a curious thing happened. The sky turned black. Dark clouds threatened rain, and I turned questioningly to my cousin.

"Ah, it won't rain," my cousin said. "Let's keep going."

I agreed, even though we had no umbrella. We didn't

want a little rain to ruin our last night of fun. But it wasn't just a little rain. A violent wind started knocking its way down the streets. Before long, we struggled to keep steady, walking like drunk men before we ever got to the bar. The rain hit then too, falling like gunfire and soaking our clothes.

The more we continued, the stronger the storm became. Finally, as we took shelter beneath an overhang, it dawned on us: maybe the storm was God's way of telling us to go home instead of trying to pursue the world's pleasures. We turned around, thrilled to have received direction from God.

That night in my room, still damp from the rain, I decided to seriously give my life to Jesus Christ and walk away from my old ways for good. But how? Suddenly, I remembered the directions of the man who shared Jesus with me out of Romans 10:9–10. It says, "If you declare with your mouth, 'Jesus is Lord,' and believe in your heart that God raised him from the dead, you will be saved. For it is with your heart that you believe and are justified, and it is with your mouth that you profess your faith and are saved." So I said it out loud!

And now, many years later, I can say that it was the best decision of my life. Once I put my trust in Jesus Christ, I started truly experiencing the goodness and beauty of His Kingdom and all the blessings that go with it. I pray that this book will highlight all the ways He has faithfully guided me and how He can do the same for you.

The Christian man who kept knocking on my door, Hugue, must have been shocked to see my cousin and I standing in church that Sunday in 1998.

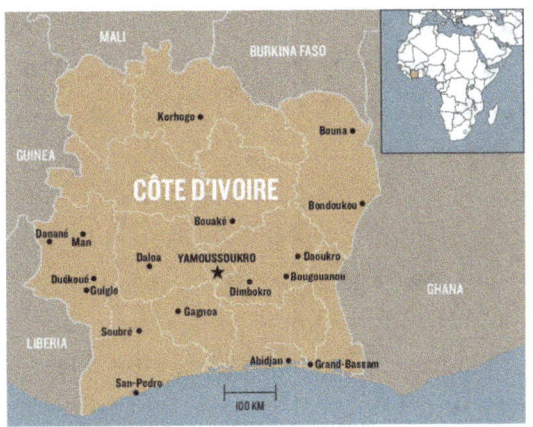

The first time Hugue asked us to come to church with him, we agreed—but only to be polite. We didn't want to hurt his feelings by giving him an outright no. But we never had the intention of attending church with him. In fact, we purposely avoided sleeping in our rooms on Saturday nights so that we could get out of hearing his knocking on Sunday morning. That way, we could act clueless when he questioned us about it later.

"No, we never heard your knocking," we would say to Hugue "truthfully" on Sunday afternoon.

But after three months, his persistence paid off. We walked through those church doors fully convinced of the presence of God after that storm, which had been strong enough to rip off several roofs in our area.

Once my cousin and I decided to attend church, I found out the most amazing thing: when I worshiped God—when I admired His character and thanked Him for all that He had given me—it felt like taking a shower. I felt clean and refreshed after!

That fresh feeling from the praise and worship of God drove me to go deeper with Him. I wanted to go deeper. I craved having my own time with Him. I found out that in the Bible, people would fast, or not eat, when they desired clearer direction or urgent provision in their life. So I started fasting like they did. More than any kind of food, I was hungry for God to move more presently in my life.

During that time I knew only this: never forget the Word of God and prayer. I would read the Bible, even when I understood little at first. When a chapter or verse spoke to me, I grabbed onto it. I made it a part of me. It became like me. Over time I started to see a greater desire for the things of God inside me. I started to feel motivated for missions, evangelizing, and leading worship.

Not too long after, a revival service came to Danané where people spoke in tongues. God had given these people the ability to speak a language they had never studied! Oh, how I longed to be able to speak in tongues! When the leaders called people up to the front for prayer, I went. They prayed for me. But nothing changed outwardly.

"Keep expecting!" they told me. "Some start speaking in tongues when they get back home. So be expecting!"

I kept that attitude of expectation. Not too long after, I attended a Christian convention in Bouaké, a city in the center of Ivory Coast, and received the gift of speaking in tongues there.

As soon as I started speaking in tongues, my life began to change. That's when the dreams began.

CHAPTER 2

A Dream of the Future

"And it shall come to pass afterward that I will pour out My Spirit upon all flesh; and your sons and your daughters shall prophesy, your old men shall dream dreams, your young men shall see visions."

—JOEL 2:28, KJV

Growing up, I never paid attention to my dreams. They didn't feel important. To this day, I don't remember a single dream before the age of eighteen.

The dreams that began after I started speaking in tongues were different. They were special, although I didn't know it initially.

In my first dream, I saw my church. We were worshipping. The whole room of people were literally bowing down in worship, and everyone was speaking in tongues. When I awoke, I didn't know what to make of the dream.

Then, a few days later, as I was leading worship, it happened! Everyone in the room bowed down exactly as I had seen in my dream. They all started worshipping in other languages.

I was stunned. I realized that the Lord had given me a dream about my future. After that, I paid remarkably close attention to what I dreamed.

CHAPTER 3

The School Dream

School in Africa is vastly different from school in America— or at least it was in the nineties. In the Ivory Coast, if you didn't pass a year, you didn't advance to the next level of education. You would repeat that year. The reason for repeating years in school varied. Sometimes you missed school because you needed to work to help your family, or sometimes you didn't have money for school supplies. Oftentimes, you would find students of different ages in the same class. For example, when I was nineteen, I was in my last year of middle school.

To enter high school, you had to pass a national exam. Your results on the exam would determine what kind of high school you would attend—and thus what kind of education you would receive. In short, the pressure was on.

Before I took the national exam in July, I prayed to do well. I wanted to secure the brightest future possible and do my best for the glory of God.

Finally, the day came when the school posted our exam results. I thought I had done well because the results on all of my pretests were positive, but I wouldn't be certain of how I ranked until I saw my name in print.

My heart started racing as I stepped into the crowd of classmates that had formed around the board with all of our names and scores on it.

But there was a problem.

My name was nowhere to be seen. A pit formed in my stomach. What had happened? What was going on? Where was my name? Everyone else saw their names posted right away. I thought I had done well, but maybe some problem would cause me to redo the entire year over.

I went home and started to seek the Lord fervently in prayer. In response, He gave me a new dream.

In the dream, I was sent to a beautiful high school, like you would find in a school in France. I knew it was a special school in the dream because much of Africa is dry, but this school's campus looked lush and green.

When I awoke, I was encouraged. If the Lord let me see the future in my dream, surely this dream would come to pass! Nevertheless, I kept the dream to myself and did not share it with others.

Three days after everyone else had seen their scores, the

school posted my name on the board. It was set apart with special gold writing because my results were so high. That dream was no mere dream! Praise the Lord!

I would be sent to a French high school in the Ivory Coast called Jean-Marie de la Mennais. My favorite part about this school was the connection it had with France: it had a program to send the best students to study in Paris. And I was determined to be the best.

As I entered the gates of Jean-Marie de la Mennais in the city of Man, it was exactly as I had seen in the dream. The dormitory buildings were beautiful and surrounded by rich, green grass. We had spacious rooms where the school hosted conferences and theater performances. It was a wonderful place to study.

Although I was on track to study in France, a riot broke out in the Ivory Coast that shut down my school for a time. I was only able to attend from 2001 to 2002.

Nevertheless, I was thankful to Jesus for the opportunity and for His faithfulness in fulfilling the dream He had placed in me.

After the riots broke out in Man, many people fled for their lives. However, I stayed nearby the city with some Christian friends. For about a year, we went around to the local villages telling people about Jesus and teaching the Bible. Then in 2003, I headed south to the coastal capital city of Abidjan. In Abidjan, I was able to continue my education, graduate from William Ponty High School in 2005, and start university the following year.

CHAPTER 4

A Wife?

A lot can happen at 2:00 a.m. Normally, people are sleeping or partying. That night, I was praying.

As you can imagine, I was asking the Lord Jesus for directions about what to do. When you've been in the middle of a national riot for several years and you don't know what to do, this is an especially good time to pray.

That night, I was also praying for my Sunday school teacher at the church in Abidjan. Specifically, I was praying for him and his fiancée as they were preparing for marriage. I was praying that they would have any darkness or confusion removed.

As I was praying for him, that's when I got a word for myself! I was shocked. I was not praying for a wife at the time, but this is what I perceived:

Your wife is going to be American.

My first response was confusion. Was I making this up? I turned to the Bible for guidance, landed on Proverbs 31:10–31 (NIV), and started reading. Here's what the passage says:

"A wife of noble character who can find? She is worth far more than rubies. Her husband has full confidence in her and lacks nothing of value. She brings him good, not harm, all the days of her life. She selects wool and flax and works with eager hands. She is like the merchant ships, bringing her food from afar. She gets up while it is still night; she provides food for her family and portions for her servant girls. She considers a field and buys it; out of her earnings she plants a vineyard. She sets about her work vigorously; her arms are strong for her tasks. She sees that her trading is profitable, and her lamp does not go out at night. In her hand she holds the distaff and grasps the spindle with her fingers. She opens her arms to the poor and extends her hands to the needy. When it snows, she has no fear for her household; for all of them are clothed in scarlet. She makes coverings for her bed; she is clothed in fine linen and purple. Her husband is respected at the city gate, where he takes his seat among the elders of the land. She makes linen garments and sells them, and supplies the merchants with sashes. She is clothed with strength and dignity; she can laugh at the days to come. She speaks with wisdom, and faithful instruction is on her tongue. She watches over the affairs of her household and does not eat the bread of idleness. Her children arise and call her blessed; her husband also, and he praises her: 'Many women do noble things, but you surpass them all.' Charm is deceptive, and beauty is fleeting; but a woman who fears the LORD is to be praised. Honor her for all that her hands have done, and let her works bring her praise at the city gate."

What confirmation! How else did I open to a passage about a godly wife right after hearing a word about my own wife? I was blown away. I asked the Lord, "She's going to be like that? Wow."

After this, I began to pay attention to the word "American" as I met new people. I did not go deeper into the meaning of the word. I didn't know whether she would be 100 percent American or partially French or something else. But I used it as a clue to know the Lord's will about the woman I was to marry.

CHAPTER 5

The American Dream

Around that time, the Lord sent me a new dream. In the dream, I saw myself going to the United States. Instead of how I normally dress, my clothes were extremely professional. My casual t-shirt and pants had vanished. I looked like a CEO in a dark, green suit. Then, I saw a team of professionals: seven women and one man. The women had beauty and class, and the man dressed like a boss. They walked towards me with purpose and the man handed me a briefcase. They told me, "We are picking you up to go to America." Then I awoke.

"How can I go there?" I asked the Lord upon waking from the dream. It seemed impossible.

Instantly, I felt the conviction that I would be like Abraham. In Genesis 12:1, the Lord told Abraham to leave his home country. As Abraham left, the Lord showed him step by step where to go and promised him a bright future. In that moment, I felt that as I made a move to leave my home, the Lord would show me where to go next.

To start the process of going, I considered studying abroad out of the country. Growing up in the Ivory Coast, French was my native language. Because of this, I looked at two French-speaking countries: Morocco and Belgium. Because going to Morocco required no visa, whereas going to Belgium did, I set my sights on Morocco. However, the first time I tried to go to Morocco, it did not work.

An elder in the church promised that he could get me a cheap ticket to Morocco through one of his connections. But that connection was not as honorable as he had thought. The money I had given for the flight was stolen! Oh, imagine the discouragement I felt.

At my lowest, the Lord encouraged me with another dream. In the dream, my friend and I shared about the Lord. He asked if I was still planning on going overseas.

"I don't know," I said.

"Don't give up," he replied. "Even if things don't happen right away, don't give up."

This dream truly encouraged me to persevere after the money for the ticket had been stolen. When I awoke, I renewed my hope of going to Morocco. I threw myself into prayer so I could understand the direction the Lord had for me. As I continued pressing on, the dreams also continued.

In one dream, I saw David Wilkerson, an American Christian evangelist! He is most well-known for his book *The Cross and the Switchblade* (1963) as well as for starting

Teen Challenge, an organization that continues to lead young people out of addiction.

In other dreams that followed, I continued to see other great people from the United States, including Condoleezza Rice, who would serve as secretary of state.

After each dream, I knew I had something great I must do in America. Why else would I be meeting great American leaders in my dreams? I knew I needed to pray to make it happen, step out like Abraham, and go.

One day, unexpectedly, a man at my church named Koffi Jean Kouamé out of nowhere offered me an opportunity to do a short-term contract with a private company to repair the interior of the roof of a five-star hotel. The roofing job paid well, and I quickly had enough money to buy a plane ticket to Morocco. The problem was I didn't have anything saved beyond that for living expenses. I did not know if I should continue trying to earn and save money in the Ivory Coast or buy the ticket to Morocco.

After I spent a good deal of time in prayer, the Lord in His goodness sent me another dream. In this dream, there were four elders. They were white as snow. They had white beards as well. I heard them say this:

"Let's pray for Thierry to finish his school in Morocco."

As I awoke, I had my answer. It was time to go to Morocco!

CHAPTER 6

Morocco

Typically, when you go to another country, you have money to spend. You have a plan. In 2010 at the age of twenty-nine, I had none of that. I just trusted that Jesus would provide based on my dream. Nevertheless, the same questions kept running through my mind, "Where am I going to sleep? How will I eat?"

Upon setting foot in Morocco, I called the youth president of the Ivory Coast, who was living in Morocco. The role of the youth president was to help students from our country adjust to life in Morocco. Now normally, he never answered the phone. But that day, God used him. He was able to put me on a bus and send me to stay with another Ivory Coast youth student.

He and his roommates were excited to welcome me.

They thought I was rich! They thought I was made of money! Because the guys welcomed me so warmly, I opened my heart to them.

"I didn't come to Morocco with financial support," I confided.

"What?!" they said. "You're crazy!"

"I think you'll have to go back to the Ivory Coast," one of them said.

The group decided that I could stay the night at least. Thankfully, my plane ticket was a round-trip ticket. So theoretically, I *could* return without too much difficulty. Nevertheless, I knew the Lord wanted me to complete my studies in Morocco. So that night, I prayed.

"What should I do?" I asked God. "If these guys don't allow me to stay with them, I don't see how I can stay in Morocco."

That night, I dreamed. In the dream, the Lord spoke back to me:

"Wait! Do not go."

After I awoke that morning, I couldn't believe what the guys told me.

"Since you're already here, don't go," they said. "You can stay with us."

Wow! The Lord had just provided me with a place to live—at least short-term. That was great news, however, I needed money to eat and to save up for my education.

In short, I needed a job. To get a "real" job in Morocco, you need to have the right paperwork—something I didn't have. The paperwork I needed was a lease with my name on it to prove I wasn't living on the streets. Without this, I could not apply for employment or to a university. So I started tutoring French. I met a rich farming family and started teaching French to their two 17-year-old sons. Although the job only brought in a small allowance, the two young men genuinely loved me as their teacher.

When their mom found out I did not have the legal paperwork I needed to work a real job in Morocco, she took compassion on me. She told me something incredible: she would write me a 10-year lease with no rent! With that, I was able to start working.

Right away, I got a job at a call center in Morocco. Even though our call center represented a French solar panel company, we took customer service calls for projects in French-speaking Canada. Because of this, my schedule was flipped to match Canadian work hours. Although the hours were different, the pay was good. God had completely provided for me financially!

CHAPTER 7

Finishing University

After several months of working at the company, my heart longed to finish my education. I asked the Lord for direction. I needed Him to guide me on what to do next, so I sought His will actively in prayer.

That's when the Lord sent me another dream. In the dream, I could see a variety of subjects floating before me. All of them started to disappear, except for one: finance. Because finance remained, I knew this was the area I was supposed to study.

But I had a problem. Although I had some money saved from the new position, I needed to be able to keep my job to survive financially. Before, I had been working night shift for our project in Canada, but then my schedule flipped to accommodate work for a company in Paris, France. I didn't see how I could work and get an education.

Again, I sought the Lord for direction. Again, He sent me a dream. In the dream, I saw a school with two entrances. One door was for students, and the other was for teachers. Also, in the dream I was well dressed, with a briefcase in my hand. I went through the door for the teachers, not the door for students.

As I awoke, I was puzzled. What did the dream mean? Was I supposed to become a teacher?

Later, at church, I had my answer. The pastor's wife had an announcement:

"For those people who are working, there's something here in Morocco called executive management training where the school allows you to continue your education and keep your day job," she said.

When I looked into the program, the timing fit perfectly with my schedule. Finally, the dream made sense. I was supposed to pursue my education through the "door" of a professional. That's how I ended up earning my finance degree in Morocco.

CHAPTER 8

Meeting My Wife

Sometimes, in praying for others, the Lord will send me a dream revealing their heart or intentions. For example, one night in Morocco I had a dream about a couple I had met at church. In the dream, the woman was crying out for a baby. She wanted to be pregnant so badly. I could feel her concern so vividly. When I awoke, I was surprised. This woman had never once mentioned to me that she wanted children. I didn't know that it was her heart's desire before the dream.

When I told her about the dream the Lord had sent me, she confirmed it was true! Sharing the dream helped her so much to see that God had heard her cries. She realized she did not need to be worried or concerned. God had heard her.

That experience helped me realize the benefit of pressing in with Jesus. In developing a prayer life, in seeking to hear from God, I could encourage others in their walk with the Lord. If you know you have a gift from God, push to develop intimacy with Him so you can grow and help others grow.

Because of that experience, I knew I could ask the Lord about a person to see their heart. Little did I know how much guidance this would give me!

My word from the Lord about an American wife came in 2003. But by the time I moved to Morocco, it was 2010. Seven years had passed. I began thinking it was possible I had misunderstood the Lord about my wife's nationality. So I started to consider the young ladies in the local Moroccan church.

One woman who I met in my customer service job stood out to me. She was attractive, and we would go to church events together. Because she was fun and seemed to love the Lord, I started to pray about whether she was the one for me. After praying seriously about her, the Lord showed me her character in a dream.

You would not believe what I saw!

In the dream, I saw she was only pretending to love God to get to me! She would come to Christian events only to impress me. Outwardly she looked good, but inwardly she was only pretending. I awoke at 5 a.m. knowing in my heart of hearts I had to cut off that relationship. I called her over the phone and ended it that morning. She cried and cried, but I was sure that God had saved my life.

Look how closely I had come to choosing the wrong

woman! Thank God, He showed me her heart. Marrying this misleading woman would have changed the course of my entire life. She could have easily derailed my walk with the Lord.

As a man, if you find yourself single with a desire to marry, start praying in your private time about the woman you have in mind. Take your possible relationship to the Lord before you ever start talking with her. Don't go quickly to talk to her. When you're young and on fire, it's much harder to hear from the Lord about the woman's character if you've already started talking to her on a relationship level. When you're already talking first, your decision-making is clouded.

If you take your possible relationship to the Lord first and get confirmation there, then you can step out in boldness, joy, and confidence. Even if she hesitates, you don't have to worry about it. And she will notice a confidence in you that will draw her to you.

Not too long after that warning dream, I met a soccer player who came to Morocco on his way to Europe. He got stuck in Morocco for a time. Every day, I shared the word of God with him, and one day, he accepted it! He gave his life to the Lord.

This soccer player was immensely popular. He had followers from all around the world. As he grew in popularity, he felt that he should use his platform to share the new joy that he found in Jesus.

Among his followers, I found my wife!

At first, when I met Isabelle online, all I knew about her was that she was a beautiful American woman. Her family had moved to the United States—specifically to the state of Georgia—from the Ivory Coast when she was young, and so she grew up speaking both French and English fluently.

Many people are from America. But of course, the clearest word I had about my future wife was this: *Your wife is going to be American.* So especially after the last woman, I started to pray in private asking the Lord whether she might be the one for me. I told her absolutely nothing about this, of course. I didn't want to force anything just because she happened to be from the United States.

After a while, I became discouraged. Isabelle was all the way across the ocean. We had never even met in person. I could tell I was more invested in the idea of our relationship than she was. I wanted her to have the same fire for me that I had for her. As I was about to give up on her, I felt a surprising answer in my heart during my prayer time: "Continue to love her."

Not long after, in 2013, one Skype call changed everything.

Isabelle announced that she would like to come see me in person. Was my computer working correctly? Did I hear her correctly? She was coming to Morocco! More important, she had the desire to come see me.

When I saw her exit the plane, I was so happy. I knew she was the one the Lord had for me to marry. During her 10-day stay in the country I proposed, and she said yes! On July 18, 2014, we married in America in her home state of Georgia.

After the ceremony, I finally worked up the courage to ask her a question that had been burning inside of me:

"Why did you choose me over all the other men in the United States?"

Her answer left me stunned.

"I had a dream," she said, smiling. "In the dream, I kept asking Father God to bring me someone who would be good for me. Then, He replied, 'You've been asking for a husband. Now I bring you someone, and you don't even want to go with him.'"

"When I woke up," Isabelle continued, "I realized that the Lord had sent you to be my husband! That's when I decided to come meet you in Morocco . . . and the rest is history."

Wow! God had been working on both of us the entire time! It blessed me to know that she carried the same fire for me that I had for her.

Isabelle is the right one for me. I know that with certainty.

She knows that with certainty. And having the Lord confirm it to both of us is such a blessing.

Oddly, the same thing happened for my friend Marie-Laure back in Ivory Coast. One day, the Lord showed her the kind of husband she would marry. He was a singer. In fact, this singer was our worship leader, Gerard! Only Gerard Kouassi was so focused on serving the Lord that his mind wasn't on her at all.

"He doesn't even look at me," she would cry.

"Stay on it," I encouraged her at the time. "If the Lord has given you this direction, keep speaking it."

Despite my advice, there came a point where she decided in her heart to give up on Gerard and go marry someone else. The very night she made that decision, God gave her a dream. It was like a movie playing out her entire future life with this other man from the beginning of the marriage to the end.

"It was horrible!" Marie-Laure said.

That awful dream encouraged her to stick to the path the Lord had shown her at first. Later, Gerard and I randomly ran into each other in Casablanca, Morocco during his time as a student in Morocco. When he saw me, he came up to me.

"Hey, I have good news for you," he said. "God has given me a wife and you know her!"

"Congratulations!" I replied. "Who is it?"

"Oh, c'mon, you know," he replied. "You know her . . ."

It was Marie-Laure! Today, the two are married with four kids.

So, when you hear from the Lord about a person, trust Him to be faithful. Continue to persevere even when it gets hard. Being with the right person makes all the difference.

CHAPTER 9

Joining the Military

After my marriage in 2014 and move to the United States, I was looking for direction in this new country. I wanted to know what I should do now. During that time of seeking the Lord gave me another dream.

In the dream, I was joining the military! The uniforms were blue. When they asked for my ID, they checked my card and simply said: "You're in."

"Just like that?" I asked.

"Yeah, you're in."

This was crazy. I didn't even have my green card yet! I wasn't even a citizen officially. Yet again, I didn't have the "right" paperwork. How could I possibly join the military of the United States if I wasn't even an official resident?

Normally, it's supposed to take roughly one to two years

to receive a green card after marrying an American citizen. Having been married in July of 2014, one would expect a green card at the earliest in August of 2015 or later in August of 2016 if things were running slowly. But the Lord expedited the process for me.

Only six months after my marriage to Isabelle, the green card arrived in our mailbox! I remember the day specifically—Saturday, January 17, 2015—because it is the date of my mother-in-law's birthday.

Normally, to get a green card, you must go to an in-person interview to verify your marriage is real in front of a government official. My wife and I never sat through a single meeting. They never even called us on the phone. I received the government's approval of our union after only one email. How great is God?

That Saturday in January, when I had my green card in hand, I marveled at how the Lord was achieving his plans in my life. That little card granted me the ability to live and work permanently in the United States. The Lord had just removed a major barrier for me to join the military!

CHAPTER 10
My First Military Connection

We don't have Thanksgiving in the Ivory Coast. The first time I celebrated the holiday, in November 2015, I was a newly married man living in America. The holiday gave the family a reason to gather together and eat turkey, mac and cheese, mashed potatoes, sweet potatoes, and, my personal favorite, apple pie.

When my brother-in-law Stephen showed up for Thanksgiving, he brought his friends as well. One of his friends, Cornell, was in the Army. When Cornell started talking about the military with me, something happened inside of me. My heart started burning! When I shook his hand, I felt an inward feeling: *Yes, go!*

It made such an impression on me that I started looking

for a recruiter the following Monday or Tuesday. He told me that I would need to pass the Armed Services Vocational Aptitude Battery (ASVAB) test, which covers a range of topics including mathematics, auto and shop information, science, mechanics, and electronics. Immediately, I went to Google to start studying for the ASVAB test by looking at old tests.

The ASVAB is an English-only test. In the Ivory Coast, I grew up only speaking French. So, I quickly understood that I needed to improve my English. As soon as I got my green card, I started looking for a job in order to improve my language skills.

One morning in January 2015, I entered Dunkin Donuts. The district manager happened to be there when I approached the counter seeking employment.

"You want to work?" he asked.

"Yes, sir!" I replied. He hired me that same day.

Although making sausage, egg, and cheese sandwiches was not my dream job, I got to talk with native English speakers every day. The work was difficult in that I needed to understand and fill orders very quickly. After three months of improving my English, I realized it was time to get a better job.

That's when I started working at the Fresh Market Supermarket. I started off in the bakery, where the manager loved me. He started putting me to work in every department. It was great to grow my vocabulary and interact with so many people. Yet I could feel a yearning inside me to improve and be a part of something bigger.

"I want to join the military," I finally told my coworkers.

"What?!" they scoffed in disbelief. "No way. The military is no joke. They don't play. How are you going to join?"

Their response stung, but their question was valid. I still needed to pass the ASVAB test. I had been studying for months to get to a point where I felt comfortable with the material and the language.

In March 2016, when I finally felt I had studied enough, I took the ASVAB with a recruiter. Immediately after, he told me that a final test would be conducted at headquarters. That first test must have been a pretest of some sort. So that same day, I went to a military base in Georgia to take the final test. The recruiter told me it would be a 300-question pass-or-fail grade so that I would know on the spot whether I passed or not.

Imagine facing a test in a foreign language with several hundred questions on it! I noticed there were questions on it that I had not even studied. I was overwhelmed. Right then, I started praying.

"I'm doing this with You!" I told the Lord.

I needed His help. God did a supernatural miracle right there because I certainly had not studied for this part of the test. Finally, the printout showed my results: PASS.

"You got it!" the recruiter said.

Praise the Lord! In that moment, I remembered how similar the events were to the dream God had given me about joining the military, and I thanked Jesus for His faithfulness.

When I told my coworkers at the Fresh Market Super-market how the test went on my next shift, they did not seem impressed. For them, joining the military wasn't a reality until I could pass basic training.

CHAPTER 11
Basic Training

took a bus from the Atlanta airport to Fort Bennett to do my basic training for the Army in September, nearly seven months after I passed the ASVAB.

During the four months of basic training the Lord gave me a new dream. In the dream, my team received an A+ at a ceremony. When I awoke, I was puzzled. I had no idea what A+ meant. In the Ivory Coast, we never received letter grades. We only received a number out of 20 points. I had no idea that an A+ was the equivalent of 20/20. I kept the dream to myself for this reason.

Only after our commander honored our platoon for our actions with a plaque, photos and medals did I share my dream with the others. They were in awe and overly excited to tell me what A+ meant. To them, it really confirmed that

I had been hearing from the Lord because I had no way of knowing what the letter indicated.

Another milestone occurred upon graduating basic training. In December of 2016 I received my American citizenship! Normally, people must wait five to 10 years after receiving their green card to become a citizen. The process speeds up for those who marry American citizens, with some waiting only three years after their green card. But I got my citizenship after just under two years! I didn't know that if you graduate from basic training, you can essentially earn your citizenship. God really provided for me.

After graduating basic training, I entered the Army National Guard Reserve. This means that you continue living at home as a civilian with drills every month to keep sharp and prepare in case of a war or national emergency.

When I visited my Fresh Market Supermarket coworkers after completing basic training, they were so surprised.

"Wow! You made it!" they said. "Congratulations! How did that happen?"

I started sharing my story about how the Lord guided my hand during the test, and it touched the store manager. After that, I experienced a higher degree of favor on the job.

In 2017, I decided to pursue Advanced Individual Training in Virginia to learn how to do my job as a 92A Logistics Specialist for the Army. When I arrived, I saw two of my buddies from Fort Bennett who knew about my dreams. They had believed me when I explained the dreams before. So, it was no surprise that they were interested when I told them my next dream.

I shared with them that I had a dream in which we climbed a mountain. On our way up, we got stuck. We were fighting to get to the top, but it was extremely difficult. Finally, exhausted, we made it to the summit. When I awoke, I understood that the "mountain" was the program we were in. It would be extremely challenging to complete the program.

My two friends believed what I had to say based on the track record of the last dream. The program did live up to the dream. It was enormously challenging. But all of us ended up completing it, just as the Lord had shown. I believe the dream was meant to encourage us to persevere even in the hardest times of the program.

In that same year, 2017, my wife received a phone call.

"I know your husband is in the military," an old friend said, "but there is oil in Texas. You can make a lot of money in oil."

He left the time and date of a job fair in Midland, Texas where people were being hired to help on oil projects. On faith, I drove from Georgia to Texas, attended the job fair, and was hired that same day! They gave me a truck and a hotel and said I could work as long as I wanted to with their project.

Although the job was extremely dangerous, it paid very well. Every day, I went to inspect the oil before it would be sold. Oil must not be mixed with water and sand if it is to be sold. Certain instruments allow you to measure these particles in the oil. Every hour, I needed to go check the oil and send that ratio to the engineer.

Although safety has been improving on-site, the job is dangerous. If there's gas, a monitor will start beeping, and you need to get away immediately. Fires, explosions, and machinery malfunctions are very real risks on the job. Nevertheless, I was able to complete my work without worrying too much about my safety, knowing that the Lord had big plans for my life.

For the next seven months I worked as many hours as possible to bring home a large income for my family. By this time, my wife and I had three children: Grace, Derrick, and Nathan. I was happy to provide for them and see some of the wealth the Lord had previously revealed I would have.

Later, the money also gave our family the ability to return to the Ivory Coast for a month to do a wedding anniversary celebration. It was special to be able to return to my home country with my family and, more important, show how faithful the Lord is. He had given me the promise of an American wife, and now my friends and family could meet her in the flesh!

When the pandemic hit in April 2020, the oil inspection job ended, and I returned home to Georgia. However, the Lord later provided me with a job at Pamarco, polishing anilox rolls for printing and manufacturing. I was thankful for the ability to continue to provide for my family, and I am excited to see where the Lord will lead me next.

CHAPTER 12

From the Heart

Your fellowship with God is precious. It's so important to deepen that relationship between you and God. Spend time in prayer. Spend time fasting. Spend time reading the Bible. Knowing God personally is not something only for the pastor; it's for you too. That relationship is a special gift that will be a blessing to you and those around you.

God has great plans for you; but when you rely on man's word, you let man talk you out of the greatness God has for you. Confiding in those who do not share that high expectation can break your faith. It will discourage you. Take my desire to join the military, for example. My coworkers at Fresh Market were not encouraging. They did not think it was possible for me to accomplish that goal. If I had listened to man's opinion of me, I would still be on aisle six. I had to disagree with their words and stand on the word of God.

The word of God shows me that God is able to overcome any problem or adversity. It encourages me to cast my cares on Him. It shows me that I am a partaker of His divine nature. And these ideas all become real to me through fellowship with Him through the Holy Spirit.

The Holy Spirit helped calm my emotions and reminded me of the power of His word. I am a part of the U.S. Army today because I trusted in God's vision for me, and I believed He could fulfill that promise.

What vision has the Lord placed in your heart? Are you letting man's opinion discourage you? My life is not over. Neither is yours. There are things the Lord wants me to do and you to do too. However, if you don't develop your relationship with God, those things may never happen. Go spend time with Him now. He's waiting with open arms. You'll never regret it!

P.O. Box 453
Powder Springs, Georgia 30127
www.entegritypublishing.com
info@entegritypublishing.com
404.472.9190